MORE!

AWESOME
JOKES

7

EVERY

VOL 2

YEAR OLD

SHOULD

KNOW!

Design: Fanni Williams / thehappycolourstudio.com
www.matwaugh.co.uk

Produced by Big Red Button Books,
a division of Say So Media Ltd.

ISBN: 978-1-912883-11-0

Published: July 2019

A note for parents and readers from the USA: I'm British. I can't help it. I'm a bloke
who goes on holiday for a fortnight, never uses a washroom and comes home knackered.
I don't have a Scooby-Doo who the Red Sox are, or what I should do with a doohickey. I've
taken out any jokes about the Queen (sorry, Ma'am), but you may still find a few that
aren't your cup of tea. The rest? Hopefully they're the bee's knees!

MORE! MORE! MORE!

AWESOME JOKES 7 EVERY YEAR OLD SHOULD KNOW!

VOL 2

MAT WAUGH

ILLUSTRATIONS BY YURKO RYMAR

Hey – you're back!

I'm sure I've met you before... Did you read the first book of Awesome Jokes? You did?

Wow, haven't you grown!

My Granny used to say that, *every* time.
I was growing of course. But I think it's mostly because she was shrinking.

Anyway, forget my Granny, and say hello to a bulging, squirming sack of jokes that I've been raising in my back garden. Expect cheeky ones, shrieky ones, and even a few sneaky ones to make you think!

Ready? It's time to pull out a wriggler, let it go and see who laughs!

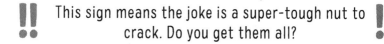 This sign means the joke is a super-tough nut to crack. Do you get them all?

PS Got your own tip-top joke? Get it on the **World Map of Awesome Jokes***!* *See page 89.*

↓ Laughs start here ↓

How do you make granny run faster?
Use hare spray!

How did Robin Hood tie his shoelaces?
With a long bow!

If the plumber ate a cheese roll on Monday and a ham roll on Tuesday, what did he eat on Wednesday?
A toilet roll!

What's the best way to send a wig?
By hairmail!

Why are small children no good at keeping secrets at the dinner table?
They keep spilling the beans!

What does a squirrel eat for breakfast?

Acornflake!

Why was the clown terrible at baseball?
He used an acrobat!

Why did the snowman miss the party?
He got cold feet!

Who's there?
Mill D.
Mill D who?
Mildew growing all over the front of your house.

What do scaredy-cat astronauts feel when they take off?
The atmos-fear!

Do you call them waterwings? Try making up a joke like this one!

Where do toddlers learn to play music?
In armbands!

How do you get off a raft?

It's as easy as falling off a log!

Where do fruit flies go to sleep?
In an apri-cot!

How are you getting on so far? Is it all making sense? Here's another one for you:

What do you call a silly sentence?
An idiom!

That's not funny, but it's true – and it's the secret to lots of jokes in this book. An idiom is a phrase or sentence that doesn't mean what it says. Work them out – or look them up – and you've got the joke!

I bet you already know hundreds of idioms. Some are **a piece of cake** (easy peasy), others are a bit more **thorny** (tricky)!

If they **drive you crazy** or some jokes in this book **have you stumped**, then **hang in there** – or maybe **sleep on it** and **pick someone's brains** tomorrow!

How do small children watch scary movies?
On the edge of their seat!

Why not?
Because if you don't, your shoes will fall off!
[You might have to think hard about this one!]

Why do woodwork fans go to play parks?
To see-saw!

**How does a farmer remember her
internet passwords?**
She keeps a secret note in her dairy!

**Which animal looks great with a diamond
waistcoat and a microphone?**
A rocking horse!

**Why is it so hard to clean out a pigsty
for the first time?**
It takes you a while to find your feet!

How do you keep
a grizzly out of
your garage?

Make it
un-bearable!

 **What type of shoes do insects wear to weddings?**
Six of the best!

Why do giraffes daydream?
Because they have their head in the clouds!

What did the mummy sunflower say to the baby sunflower?
It's time to rise and shine!

'This new cardboard mousetrap can catch anything!' said the adverts, and they were right – it caught fire!

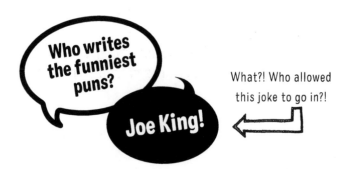

Who writes the funniest puns?

Joe King!

What?! Who allowed this joke to go in?!

What's the easiest thing to catch in winter?
A cold!

**Which type of racing car driver always
wins at Tic Tac Toe?**
Autocross!
*[In Britain we call this game Noughts and Crosses.
I don't, because then the joke doesn't work!]*

What do you call a dizzy pilot?
Flight headed!

**What did the buffalo bellow as he
dropped his calf off at buffalo school?**
Bison!

**If you drop a brick on your foot, how
do you get to hospital?**
By car. Or Toe Bus.

What do you call a slow eagle?
A soar loser!

What do you call a man who runs a glue factory?
A stick man!

Why did the little boy leave dog biscuits outside his door?
His Dad said you should always think about the paw people.

Where do bees get off?

At the buzz stop!

How does a footballing bear move teams?
He applies for a trans-fur!

How do you tell a puffer fish bad news?
Let him down gently!

What makes camel racing so dangerous?
Speed humps!

What do you call a cow in space?
Untouch-a-bull!

What do you call a cow with a rocket up its bottom?
Unstopp-a-bull!

What do you call a cow that's…umm…ahh…
Forgett-a-bull!

What do you call a cow that won't stand still?
Uncount-a-bull!

**What's a cow's favouri
clothes shop?**
Anywhere suit-a-bull!

**What do you call a cow
that will also round
up sheep?**
Convert-i-bull!

(ARE YOU HAVING A CALF?)

What do call cow with six legs playing the bagpipes?
Improb-a-bull!

What do you call a cow that goes backwards?
Revers-i-bull!

What do you call a cow on your sofa?
Uncomfort-a-bull!

What do you call a cow that can't decide if it's male or female?
Mum-bull!

How does a cat make milkshakes?
Using its whiskers!

This tea is weak. Can I have some of yours?
No way – it's *MIGHTY!*

What do you call a fold-up desk for grooming cats?
Paw-table!

I only ordered this starter five minutes ago but it's here already. That's what I call souperfast!

When my sister sucks a lemon, she pulls a funny face. But when my dad blows a raspberry, we all pull a funny face!

What do you call a small child with nits?
Baby buggy!

How does a farmer count sheep?

With a baaa chart!

What does a percussionist put on her pizza?
Bell peppers!

Knock, Knock!
Who's there?
Stega!
Stega who?
Stegasaurus, and now he knows where we live!

What did the prisoner give the judge as he was sentenced?
A cheeky crime wave!

How did the farmer cross his flooded field?
By hedgerow!

What do you call a bird that can dance?
A jig-gull!

What about a running bird?
A jog-gull!

And what do you call a bird that can keep three balls in the air?
A jug-gull!

Why do the police use sniffer dogs?

Because a dog nose best!

Waiter, Waiter!

There's a bug crawling across my lunch!
You're right sir. I don't want to interrupt him while he's on a roll.

A polar bear walks into a shop.
A bottle of...

...

...

...

lemonade, please.
Why the big paws?

What do rock stars play when they go skydiving?
An air guitar!

!! **Why is an old man's face like a newspaper?**
They both have huge headlines! **!!**

How do giraffes race?

Neck and neck!

Knock Knock!
Water!
Water who?
Water you messing about at, open the door!

Which fruit has the sharpest taste?
A pear of scissors!

Why was the chicken footballer sent off?
For fowl play!

How does an eagle go backwards?
It uses its wing mirrors!

How can you tell if a skeleton has a cold?
Listen to his coffin!

Can I give you a tip?
Absolutely sir, I'd be delighted.
Get a better chef.

How does a dolphin buy fish online?
Point and click!

What do you call a wee by your new dog?
Pup-pee!

What do you call a baby's wee?
Nap-pee!

What wee would you have if you drank washing up liquid?
Soapee!

What do you call a trip to the toilet when you're crying?
Weepee!

Knock Knock!

Who's there?
Hoof!
Hoof who?
Hoo-forgot to leave the door open?

What's scarier than a UFO in your garden?
A flying saucer in your kitchen!

Which dinosaur makes the worst pet?
T Wrecks!

What game do ducks play with their ducklings?
Beak-a-boo!

How do acrobats start their rehearsals?

With a roll call!

There's too much sea salt on this dish.
That's not sea salt, sir – the chef has dandruff.

**What do rally drivers say as they start
the vacuum cleaner?**
Eat my dust, sucker!

Why are there so many librarians in prison?
Because they always get the longest sentences!

**What's the easiest way to avoid
sharing your pizza?**
Put anchovies on it, of course!

Who's there?
Busted!
Busted who?
Bus didn't come,
now I'm late for school!

You must be joking!

Humph... this section makes me grumpy. Since Book 1, seven year olds from around the world have been sending me their jokes. I wouldn't mind because I love getting emails. But the problem is... THEY'RE FUNNY.

This is not how it's supposed to work. Grown-ups know best. Grown-ups *are* the best. Just leave the funnies to me, OK? 😠

GEORGE FROM GLEN ELLYN, USA

What did one eye say to the other eye?

Between you and me, I smell something!

JEREMY & ZOE FROM SAN FRANCISCO, USA

What did the ornament say to the Christmas tree?

Can we hang?

What did zero say to eight?

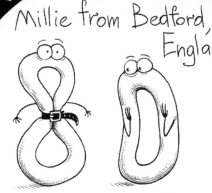

Millie from Bedford, England

Wow, your belt's too tight!

ROSINA FROM MAIDSTONE, UK

Have you heard of the boy who ate a lot of nuts?

He BECAME nuts!

AVA FROM BALTIMORE, USA

Where do pencils go for vacation?

Pencilvania!

ELIZA FROM BURGESS HILL, UK

What do giraffes draw on?

A leaflet!

Knock, knock!
Who's there?
Peas!
Peas who?
Peas stop knocking!

Teddy from
Atlanta, USA

What do you get when you cross a pig with a dinosaur?

Jurassic Pork!

What's a bean that walks and talks?

A human bean!

BRIAN FROM TUAMGRANEY, CO CLARE, IRELAND

What do you say to a hyena if you meet one in the forest?

Hi-ena!

Do you have a great joke? Get it on the **World Map of Awesome Jokes** – see page 89!

LOUIS FROM THAMES DITTON, UK

How do you make your teeth go red?

You blush your teeth!

CACHE FROM TUCSON, USA

Why are cats so religious?

Because they always say their purrs!

AMELIA FROM CHARLOTTE, USA

What did the chicken say when he got sick?

I have chicken bocks!

Knock Knock!

Who's there?
No fin!
No fin who?
No fin to eat, no fin to drink –
I'm starvin!

Knock Knock!

Who's there?
Some fin!
Some fin who?
Some fin in there smells good,
now open the door and let me in!

What did one eel say to the other?

You sure are electro-cute!

Knock Knock!

Who's there?
Any fin!
**Oh no, not you again! OK…
Any fin who?**
Any fin will do, if you don't
let me in soon I'll eat the
doormat!

Why did Arthur wear armour over his pyjamas?
He was on a knight shift!

Which fish has the biggest fin?
The great height shark!

How do the Christmas elves answer the register?
Present, Santa!

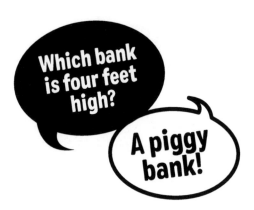

When is a shark attack not a shark attack?
When he's just pulling your leg!

What do you call a jacket on fire?
A blazer!

Why will the pandas get a surprise at teatime?
Bam *BOO!*

What would you be if you could capture all the methane that comes out of cows' bottoms?
Stinking rich!

Who's there?
Wiser man!
Wiser man who?
Wiser man taking away
your car?

**How does a pig with a broken leg
get around?**
In a squeal-chair!

Where do toads put their coats?
In the croak-room!

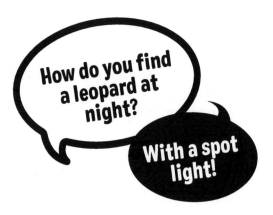

How do you find a leopard at night?

With a spot light!

 **I ate my dog's dinner and now I don't feel very... BLEURRRGH!**
I was afraid you might bring that up.

What did the farmer say when his chicken laid an egg the size of a football?
How irr-egg-ular!

How do you know when the storm is over?
Listen for the thunder claps!

Why do eagles like sitting on church spires?
Because they're birds of pray!

Why is 'w' the most delicious letter?
It's the difference between eating a doughnut hole and a doughnut whole!

Where do owls go for fun?
To the hooting range!

What's the best way to give someone a microphone for their birthday?
Put it in rapping paper!

What did Rudolph wear to the party?
A rein bow!

Why couldn't the fox catch the sheep?
The sheep were on flock down!

Why are clockmakers so rude?

They're always making faces!

Which drum should you never hit with a stick?
Your ear drum!

What do you get after you've been playing in rockpools?
Clammy hands!

What's the meanest thing in the kitchen?
A pinch of salt!

What do you call a musical fish?
A piano tuna!

Why did the mummy kangaroo have a bad back?
Because her baby joeys wouldn't get out of bed!

This fish is absolutely swimming in grease!
Goodness me, you're right, sir. It's not even supposed to be alive.

What do you call it when your Dad changes the bedding in a flash?
Sheet lightning!

What do you call a stork that flies into a door?

A dork!

Did you hear about the twins who couldn't sit nicely on a roller coaster?
They fell out!

Did you hear about the architect who was sacked for looking out of the window?
His boss said he had to draw the line somewhere!

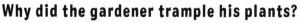

Why did the gardener trample his plants?
He was just killing thyme!

THERE'S NO SHAME IN THESE NAMES..

These are some of the trickiest jokes to get in this book. Give yourself a new superhero name if you can understand them all!

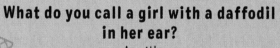

What do you call a girl with a daffodil in her ear?
April!

What do you call a boy that's good at treading water?
Bobby!

What do you call his friend who swims with one arm in the air?
Finn!

What do you call a bright boy?
Sonny!

What do you call a boy that lives underground?
Cole!

What do you call a girl who loves popcorn?
Maisy!

What do you call a girl who'll tell you a story?
Paige!

What do you call a girl who changes colour at bedtime?
Skye!

I'm so hot! I can't cool down! I'm roasting!
Calm down and take a chill pill!

What do you call a lamb that looks like its mother?
Ewe-thful!

Why did the nervous carpenter visit the dentist?
He'd been chewing his nails!

How do sheep get to the moon?

They hit the space baa!

Why should you beware of men with big boots?
In case they add you to their stamp collection!

Who's there?
Howl!
Howl who?
How'll you know unless you
open the door?

**What button does a hungry airline
captain press?**
Automatic Pie-lot!

What does a llama do when you tell him a joke?
He spits his sides!

 **Someone's put glue on my coffee cup! Is there anything I can do?**
Not really. Just keep a stiff upper lip, there's a good chap.

What do ghosts play in old, haunted houses?
Draughts!

Why was the skeleton tired?
He was dead on his feet!

What did the lifeguard do when he lost his binoculars?
Took a long pier instead!

I've planted a coin because I'm trying to grow a money tree.
You should be sow lucky!

Why did the man wake up next to a pile of pancakes?
He'd been tossing and turning in his sleep!

We were burgled last night, and now I can't wash.
Why not?
Because the robber decided to take a bath!

Waiter, Waiter!

Why is the bill covered in scraps of ground meat?
That's your complementary after-dinner mince, sir.

What happened to the man who fell into the coffee machine?

He came to a bitter end!

What do you call a mean fishmonger?

Sell-fish!

What do you call vegetables that grow at night?

Moonbeans!

What about in the day?

Sunbeans! [I think you could guess that one!]

Knock Knock!

Who's there?
Toucan!
Toucan who?
Toucan play your game, so who are you?

How do turkeys drink Coke?

From a goblet!

I've completely lost my appetite!
Here, take this nosebag.
Will it help?
Definitely. You'll soon be eating like a horse!

What do you call a boy who keeps chocolates in his underwear?
Smartie pants!

FIND A RING, FIND A JOKE!

What do you call a ring that's too hot to wear?
Sear-ring!

What do you call a ring you lose in the washing?
Launder-ring!

What do you call a ring you lose in the cake mix?
Stir-ring!

What do you call a ring that appears by magic?
Conjur-ring!

What do you call a ring with a diamond the size of a football?
Stagger-ring!

 **I can't stop repeating myself and I'm sick of the sound of my own voice!**
You can say that again!

What do you call a clown who's lost his trousers?
A comic strip!

What do you call a dangerous blue lizard?
A blizzard!

What's the best way to climb over a hedge?

With stile!

Tricky, but think about the spelling!

What type of criminal wears protective glasses to make an omelette?
A safecracker!

 **I'm addicted to crossword puzzles! What's wrong with me?**
I'm sorry, I haven't a clue!

If you jump out an aeroplane with a piano, what should you play first?
A rip chord!

How do slugs train for the army?
On assault course!

Waiter, Waiter!

This chicken curry is still frozen!
You did request extra chilly, sir!

Why does Dracula's mum always carry a credit card?
Because every time she pays with cash she loses Count!

What do you call a puppy who lives on the back seat?
A carpet!

How do you remind a musician?
With a sticky note!

Why do thieves always win?
Because every time they enter,
they take first prize!

**Which sense do parents lose
every morning before school?**
Their sense of humour!

Why doesn't Arthur go to war on Saturday or Sunday?
Because he only fights on weak knights!

Waiter, Waiter!

I asked for a pie, but this one is small and old!
Yes sir, it's a cottage pie!

Why did the silly boy get wet every time it rained?
Because his mother was always encouraging him to stand out!

Why did the snowman upset his friend?
He gave her the cold shoulder!

DOCTOR, DOCTOR!

I'm a teacher and I can't stop correcting everything!
You'll feel better soon – mark my words!

This water jug makes a knocking sound when you pour it!
Yes sir, you asked for tap water.

What do angry people do to relax?
Crossword puzzles!

How did the race in Death Valley end?
In a dead heat!

How does a comedian make an omelette?
She starts with a few wisecracks!

What's the easiest way to save money on your birthday?
Cut the cake!

Did you hear about the lion who sells sunglasses on the beach?
He's doing a roaring business!

Which is a teacher's favourite tree?
Poet-tree!

Did you hear about the thieves who kept their stolen goods in a diamond chest?
Police say it's a very hard case to crack!

I have a memory like a sieve!
Can you pop along to the kitchen then, please?
Will that help?
No, but I need to drain some carrots.

What do you call a frog astronaut?
A space hopper!

I've got my hand stuck in this magic lamp. Will it ever come out?
You wish!

My new kitten eats when I eat, sleeps
when I sleep.
I think she's a copycat.

**What did the dad say to the boy with
a bone on his head?**
You can't go out dressed like a dog's dinner!

Why is it easy to find a tree surgeon?
They have branches everywhere!

**Did you hear about the criminals who stole a
truckload of bananas?**
They gave police the slip!

What's a
cat's favourite
country?

Lapland!

Did you hear about the strawberries who got stuck in a jam?
Police told them to spread out!

How did the boys make up after their argument about who broke wind?
One of them offered to clear the air!

What do you call a man with three legs, five nipples, and seven toes on one foot?
Very odd looking!

What breakfast do spies eat?

Scrambled eggs!

What's the scientific name for snoring?
Sound asleep!

DOCTOR, DOCTOR!

I feel like I'm trapped at the bottom of a well!
You'll have to speak up, I'm afraid!

What do you call a sheep and a cow who have popped out for a walk?
A nice ram-bull!

My jumper had a small hole in it this morning, and now it's massive.
I told you, sew!

When does a ray of light hurt your eyes?
When it's a sting ray!

DOCTOR, DOCTOR!

Every time I sneeze my friends say they need a shower, but I don't understand why!
Hmm... The answer is on the tip of my tongue!

 **I feel like a roller coaster! Is that normal?**
Absolutely. We all have our ups and downs.

Why couldn't the conker go to choir?

He was a hoarse chestnut!

What did one knife say to the other?
Hey, you're looking sharp!

Why do parents hate ironing?
Because it always increases!

What do you call a boat full of all your grumpy aunts and uncles?
A terrible relation-ship!

What do you call a man in a bank with a balaclava?
Robin!

What did the sheep say when she saw the green field?
Ooh look, a salad baa!

**I made a cake on the kitchen table.
I ate dinner at the dining table.
I put my drink on the coffee table.
So why did Mum go crazy when I made a salad on her dressing table?**

 **My Grandad's in a wheelchair and doesn't feel well. Is he OK?**
Yes, but I think he might go downhill fast.

How did the skydiver meet his wife?

He fell in love!

How does a toddler count cakes?
One, two, free for all!

 **How do tiny bees get to school?**
On a mini buzz!

Why are glue thieves so hard to catch?
They'll always stick to their story!

8 JOKES ABOUT HOSPITAL WARDS...

Where do they put hungry hospital patients?
Stew-ward!

...what about the women?
Stew-wardess!

...and where do they put patients they can't cure?
Awk-ward!

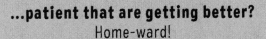

...patient that are getting better?
Home-ward!

...and the ones that aren't?
Down-ward!

DOCTOR, DOCTOR!

Every time I leave the house I get chilly knees! What should I do?
Oh pull your socks up!

...patients on a month-long diet?
Fast four-ward!

...patients that keep coming back?
Re-warded!

...patients called Ed?
Ed-ward! [THAT'S ENOUGH WARD JOKES!]

How did the frog leave the restaurant?
He tip-toad out!

Why do beekeepers sleep so well?
Because they always have sweet dreams!

What is a cat's favourite party game?

Sardines!

What does an orchestra play at the interval?
Musical chairs!

What does a mummy vampire say to a baby vampire who won't eat?
Suck it and see!

Why couldn't the gardener hear very well?
He'd forgotten to take his earwigs off!

You find a man in the desert who hasn't had a drink in three days. What should you give him?
Thirst aid!

Why don't hats last forever?

Because people wear them out!

How do bats raise a toast?
Bottoms Up!

My uncle stopped washing ten years ago to save money on soap.
How is he now?
Filthy rich!

My wife is an astronaut, so she's always going away with work.
Does she mind?
Not at all, she's over the moon!

Here's one for Roald Dahl fans...
Why did George feel so strange?
Someone gave him a taste of his own medicine!

Why do apples like skydiving?
Because they're hard core!

Which pudding is brown and lives in the woods?
A chocolate moose!

Why is the letter D always a bad sign?
Because it's at the end of the worl**d**!

What do you get if you run behind an old car?

Exhausted!

Did you hear about the boy wizard who turned his teacher into a chicken?
He's been eggs-spelled!

My mum said my bedroom was filthy and smelly.
What did you say?
I said she shouldn't use dirty words!

How can you tell when a river is angry?
It's foaming at the mouth!

 **I can't sleep since I lost my white rabbit!**
Here, borrow my magic wand.
That should do the trick.

What's worse than butterflies in your tummy?
Caterpillars up your nose!

What's worse than finding sand in your armpit?
Finding an arm in your sandpit!

What's the best way to store your vegetables?
In a leek-proof container!

DOCTOR, DOCTOR!

My baby looks like a goat.
You've got to be kidding!

Did you hear about the man who went to the doctor because his glasses kept falling off?
He was diag-nosed!

Why don't centipedes drive cars?
They can never find one with enough legroom!

Why do nervous actors eat so much spinach?

For the butterflies in their tummies!

Why do bad sailors make too much food?
They're always going overboard!

Why do tree surgeons make great actors?
Because every day they take a bough!

 **I've been hit by a car. I have two broken arms, a broken leg, three cracked ribs and tyre tracks on my face.**
You should take a holiday.
How will that help?
It sounds like you're feeling a little run down!

 **Who's there?**
Meaty.
Meaty who?
Meteor coming, everybody in the cellar!

How do you find a place to store your wigs?

Use your head!

Why do slugs make terrible actors?
They don't like to be seen in the slimelight!

DOCTOR, DOCTOR! **Did you hear about the centipede who has spent his whole life putting on ice skates?**
They say he's on his last legs!

 **I can't get to sleep!**
Try the roof. You'll soon drop off.

**What's the best way to keep your
baggy swimming shorts up?**
Use a life belt!

**If you ride your bike to the shops,
why should you always ride back?**
Because recycling is good for the environment!

My Dad went to buy some dumbbells last week. He wanted to try them out before he bought them, but he was arrested for shoplifting!

 What do you call a house made out of straw?
A lighthouse!

What do you call a boy who munches his bogeys?
A picky eater!

What do you call someone with 14 fridges?
A fridge magnet!

Who helps an orchestra to play fast music?
The lightning conductor!

My brother eats his food off the floor and goes crazy for sugar lumps.
My Mum says he eats like a horse!

I got a letter today. The postman bowed as he gave it to me, and told me I looked great. It must have been sent by first class male.

What do you call cheap biscuits for dogs?

Paw quality!

My Dad says it's OK to skip to school and skip home again. So why do I get told off as soon as I skip class?

 What weather makes archery impossible?
Mist!

 **I've spilled superglue on my hands!**
Hmm. I can book you into hospital next week, they may be able to help.
Next week? What will I do until then?
Keep your fingers crossed!

Have you seen that new movie about the submarine?
I've heard it's deeply moving!

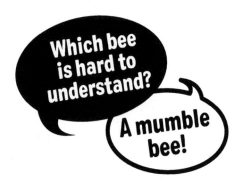

Which bee is hard to understand?

A mumble bee!

What's the best way to check if your bacon is ready?
Use a magnifrying glass!

You put pumpkins in a pumpkin pie and cherries in a cherry pie – so where should you put magnets?
In a magpie!

What's the easiest way to make friends?
Use modelling clay!

How do you describe a dancer with illuminated shoes?
Light on his feet!

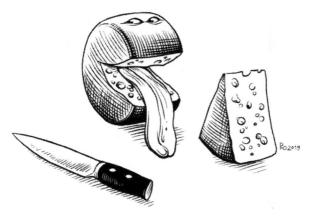

Why did the cheese stick its tongue out?
It wasn't very mature!

How do you know whether it's going to be rainy or whether it will be cold?
Check a whether map, of course!

How do astronomers like their coffee?
The Milky Way!

I got nine marks out of ten on my spelling test, but my teacher says I have to take it again.
Why?
They were all question marks!

How does a mouse call his mum?

With a micro phone!

My uncle is a carpenter and for my birthday he gave me a personalised ruler.
Does it suit you?
Oh yes – it's made to measure!

What's the worst way to start keeping piranha fish?
Dip your toe in!

 **I can't turn my head!**
Don't worry, you have a lot
to look forward to!

Why did the clown stop doing his act backwards?
Because the audience couldn't see the funny side!

How does a monk open a monastery door?
With his monkey!

Did you hear about the man who fell into the glue machine?
He came to a sticky end!

What type of tree can you eat?

Pastry!

What's a window cleaner's favourite motto?
No pane, no gain!

How did the baker fix his bread machine?
With dough nuts!

Where do lambs watch sheep on skateboards?
On EweTube!

**Whenever my brother goes to someone's birthday,
he needs the toilet.**
He's a party pooper!

**Whenever my sister goes to someone's birthday,
she eats until she's ready to burst.**
She's a party popper!

What do you call a colander made of gold?
Expen-sieve!

... what about a 10ft colander?
Impress-sieve!

... or one for draining sprouts?
Repul-sieve! [You can make your own jokes from now on!]

Where do French cats swap gossip?

In a chat-room!

Makes no sense?
Find a French
speaker!

What do you call a bicycle for beginners?
A trycycle!

Why is the world's strongest man always so popular?
Because everywhere he goes he pulls a crowd!

Why don't sharks have hair?
Because they've all gone fin on top!

**My name is Jack and I lick ice creams.
What about you?**
Isaac!

How do acrobats fall in love?
Head over heels!

**Did you hear about the thief who forgot his gloves
on a chilly night?**
He was caught red handed!

I'm having real trouble finishing this story.
Don't worry, your first draft will blow them away!

Why do artists make very poor witnesses?
Because their memory is so sketchy!

Why can't you trust a sheep?

They'll always try to fleece you!

How did the giant break into the castle?
Threw the gates!

Why do dominoes never break the rules?
Because they always fall in line!

How does a photographer find the best water slide?
Point and chute!

What kind of music do surgeons like?
Anything with a loud heart beat!

What shaped hole do escaping parrots make?

Polly gone!

Why was the doctor dismissed?
He kept losing his patients!

How do you become a great baker?
Prove yourself!

Did you hear about the joke writer who ran out of jokes?
YOU HAVE NOW!

Now it's your turn!

Writing jokes is simple, isn't it? You just think of something funny!

But that's where it gets a bit tricky, because people laugh at different things depending on their background, mood and lots of other things you can't control. If you've ever said the most hilarious thing possible and people look like you've just made a horrible smell, then you know what I mean!

But don't worry – if you make up a joke that gets *most* people chuckling, you've got a good one.

So then: would you like the chance to show the world how hilarious you are? Let's go!

If you already have a humdinger, then read on. But if you fancy writing your own, and you like drawing too, then get your thinking cap on and your pencils ready, and turn to page 90!

I know a great joke!

If you're sitting on a zinger, there are two possibilities:

1 – your bottom is a bit itchy
2 – you already have a brilliant, clever and super funny joke.

If it's number 1, I recommend that you see a doctor, pronto.

If it's number 2, then send your joke to me and I'll put it on my **World Map of Awesome Jokes**!

Head over to the map now to discover silly jokes, clever jokes and weird jokes. Some jokes rhyme, some are a crime, but they're all sent in by children like you!

Could you be the first on the map from your town?

et a grown-up to send in your joke:
www.matwaugh.co.uk/jokemap

Jokers wanted!

Could you write and illustrate your own joke?

There are lots of different types of jokes. Many jokes use *surprise*. Think about this classic (not one of mine!):

> **What's brown and sticky?**

The first time you heard this you were probably thinking of all the brown, sticky and smelly things in the world! But here comes the answer:

> **A stick!**

Surprise! It's not rude at all, and now you're thinking about how you've been tricked by two meanings of the word 'sticky'. It's a very clever joke.

So let's try something easier: a pun. Puns are great fun for kids because the sillier they are, the better! Here's how it works. Start with a great word: **humbug**. In Britain, a humbug is a type of hard, minty sweet or candy (yummy). But what does humbug *sound* like? It sounds like a joke!

> ### What do you call an insect that doesn't know the words?
> A humbug!

That's just the start. Find humbug rhymes – even if they're not real words – and you can make lots *more* jokes!

How? Just go through the alphabet letter by letter, changing the first sound (ignore the vowels: a, e, i, o & u).
· Don't forget that some sounds are made up of more than one letter, like *cr-*, *ch-* and *th-*.
· If you're feeling adventurous, you can use 'nearly' rhymes, too. As long as the word sounds similar, it's good!

Let's try it out with **h**umbug:

b➤ **b**umbug. Oops, what a way to start: I made a rude word! I won't use that one or I'll be in trouble!

c➤ **c**omebug. That's good! Let me think...

> ### What do you call an obedient insect?
> A comebug!

Not bad, but I bet you can do better! What about *chumbug*, or *crumbug*? *Dumbug*? It's your turn!

How did you get on? Have you invented a brand new bug joke?

Great! Now every awesome joke needs a fantastic illustration, just like the ones in this book by super-clever Yurko. He's really thought about the jokes, and added lots of extra detail to make them even funnier.

So now you can do the same. Use the page opposite to tell and draw your bug joke, and don't forget to make that picture really funny!

If you'd like a bigger sheet to draw on, you can download one to print out at *matwaugh.co.uk/wall*

Happy? Ask a grown-up to take a picture and send it to jokes@matwaugh.co.uk – I'll put all the best ones on the **Wall Of Awesome Jokes** on my website.

Happy bug hunting!

Parents: see the website for full terms and conditions.

My Awesome Joke!

Question: _____

_____

_____

Answer: _____

My illustration:

My first name: _____ **Age:** _____

Home town and country: _____

Hello! Tell your mum you
don't need an eye test, yours
are working very well.

Phew, we're done!

Reviews of joke books are almost as funny as the books themselves.

You're not funny!
These jokes are too old!
These jokes are for babies!
These jokes are too rude!

I get all of those and I don't mind: it just shows that everyone is different! But if you have something nice to say about this book, or you're just really funny – then please pop over to Amazon with your parent and write something about this book so others know what to expect.

As long as you found something to laugh about, I'm happy too!

About Mat Waugh

In the first book, I told you about my batty aunt. Here are some new things about me.

I have big crow's feet. I know what you're thinking – how do I buy my shoes? But crow's feet are those wrinkles that grown-ups get next to their eyes.

Some people get crow's feet because they need glasses but don't wear them enough (true).

Some people get them because their skin doesn't have enough oil, called sebum. I only included this fact because then I can write the word *see-bum*. (What?! That's how you say it!).

But I get crow's feet because I spend a lot of time squinting at my three children, trying to give them Paddington hard stares. They ignore me.

I've jumped out of a plane, done bungee jumps and tried wreck diving. I even met Mrs Waugh at a theme park. But last week I got dizzy on the trampoline. The lesson? **Never get old, children!**

I still can't do handstands. I'm practising.

I produce enough dribble each day to fill a water bottle, and enough each year to fill the bath.*

My favourite sounds are birdsong, tapping keys, and windmills.

When I was 19 I had a ticket for a flight with some friends, but there wasn't enough space. The airline put us on a tiny plane instead and I sat in the co-pilot's seat. While my friends were sleeping in the back, the pilot let me have a go at flying the plane.

I've taken a photo of my daughters every single Sunday since they were born. I'm very proud of this, as I'm not very good at homework. In nearly every photo, they're pulling a silly face at me.

Finally, I love getting emails (but ask your parents first!). You can reach me here: mail@matwaugh.co.uk

* So do you!

Three more to try!

Cheeky Charlie series
Meet Harriet and her small, stinky brother. Together, they're trouble. Fabulously funny stories that will keep you snorting way past bedtime.

Fantastic Wordsearches
Wordsearch with a difference: themed, crossword clues and hidden words await!

The Fun Factor
When the fun starts vanishing from Thora's village, she's the only one to notice. Frosty the headmaster is definitely up to no good, but what about Dad's new girlfriend? A mystery adventure story for gadget-loving kids aged 8+.

Available from Amazon and local bookshops.

Be the first to know about new stuff! Sign up for my emails at matwaugh.co.uk

Printed in Great Britain
by Amazon

69457950R00061